Me & Her

Takira Harris

BookLeaf Publishing

India | USA | UK

Presentation by *BookLeaf Publishing*

Web: www.bookleafpub.com

E-mail: info@bookleafpub.com

ISBN: 9789358315943

First edition 2024

Girl

After I am sent back for the third time
After I watch the video, hear the laughs, throw
up again, and wish my friends a happy holiday
What will I be
I am not okay, not happy, not relieved, not
myself
I suppose I'm just a teenaged girl tries
continuously to leave behind everything I know
because the world is not kind enough to me
I am not kind enough to me
So, I will continue to suffer, for awhile
I'll pretend he didn't record me, that they didn't
laugh watching the video back, that the medics
didn't take me back upstairs, and that my family
knowns what's best for me
I will pretend until I've made a home in myself
and created a love so strong and so deep for
myself that'll I never have to pretend again
Not like that
Never again

Locked Inside and Out

Being locked outside of your body
Outside of your love
Outside of your family
Outside of your life
Outside of your mind
Not knowing where to go next
What to be next
Who to be next
When's the next time I'm going to smile
When's the next time I'm going to laugh
When's the next time I'm going to get hurt
When's the next time I can leave this place
I want to leave my body
I want to leave this earth
There's nothing here for me
Nothing I can hold on to
I should've made deeper connections
Ones that can't be paved over by a few weeks
I want to be deeper
I want to become one with the earth
Then I'll have a purpose
There'll be no maybes only certainty
I can't read my own mind
I can't see my future
My past is murky

I wish I could go
Not back not forward
Never put a lock on yourself I did once and it
killed me

Not the End

If I soak these sheets
Will they be scared
Will they ask why I did it
Will some know
Will some care
After 5 years I know there will not be some that
care
All will care they always have and they always
will
But even if they didn't I do
Now

There's Always Somewhere

How long until I get new skin
When will I shed
In my dreams when I choose to live, I envy
myself
How can't she see her future
Maybe she's hoping for the best
I hoped for the best with the boxes
I packed and packed but had nowhere to go
If I don't pack, I won't be ready for the move
I have to build strength
So, when I have the chance I will take it without
a second thought
I do not have the strength to miss an opportunity
I don't think that I'd ever be able to forgive
myself
I wanted to go faster ahead to the better
Too much time has passed I have learned to wait
and to move when it originates in the heart.

To Be Seen

It is the most amazing feeling in the world to be
seen
To have someone who knows your soul and puts
in effort to grow with your soul
What I have was not predestined
It couldn't have been
I hope in every life that I have her there to see
my soul
Maybe in another life you would see my soul
and you wouldn't like it
I would risk it, put everything on the line in any
universe, if it meant I would have other
opportunities to have you as my best friend
You can call me greedy because I already know I
am
To be seen by a best friend is everything
My life experience would not be complete
without her

The Greatest Gift

It's been a month a long hellish month
Things keep piling on top of one another, one
second I think it's fine then it's not
I'm quiet because those who I want to care the
most don't hear me they see me but don't hear
me
I see my life on repeat the same things
happening over and over try and change them
I tell myself that I can't
Maybe if I'm quiet, maybe if I don't say anything
at all, maybe if I don't talk about, it will change
itself
Maybe I'll stay quiet until you can hear me until
you can see me with everything that I am and
am not

Horrible Dreams

STOP RUNNING
I'm begging myself to stop running, but I can't
I have to slam into myself to stop me, to warn
me
Something terrible has happened I can hear
myself whisper
I can feel the sweat running down my neck
before I fall into myself and collapse on to
myself in an infinite loop
I'm not breaking the loop I keep repeating it
I'm failing every chance I get to be better
What if I escaped off a cliff
The second the thought leaves my mind I'm
running again and I can't stop
I'm at the cliff and I'm falling
Even as I'm screaming, and I can't stop thinking
But now my back is breaking in half, and I'm
being stabbed in the back
By myself?
Did I make things worse, or did I break the
loop?

Not Mine

I've longed for things that I cannot have
I cannot have them because I am not good
enough?
I cannot have them because I am cursed?
Because bad things always happen to me?
I cannot have them because I don't know how to
take care of them
Keep them alive
I want to stop plucking pretty little things from
the ground because I feel I deserve them
I am not entitled to these things I don't think
anyone is and no one should be
I will learn to leave the pretty little things where
they are
When I feel overwhelmed with a sense to pluck
them from the earth
I will think about how it would feel to be taken
from everything, life shorted, and adored for
seemingly seconds of my life because of an
unrequited love

Who Is Here for Me?

I hear crying
My face is wet too, pooling out of my eyes are
tears that I promised I would only shed when I
am alone
But I am never alone
I hear footsteps now and my sobs are getting
heavier
I don't want anyone to feel like that
I have to suck up my tears I'm here to console
another
She has slowed down and as I'm standing right
behind her I feel her turn around and I'm
compelled to do the same
I turn around and it is me
I turn back towards the girl I came to console,
and she is gone
There's a tap on my shoulder and I know she is
here for me
I'm here for her but who is here for me
Is it you or is it me?

Boundaries

There was a word that once scared me
It starts with the letter b
When I used to hear this word, I would freeze
My body would get cold, the gooseflesh would
arrive, and a thought would crawl right behind
my eyes and put a filter over everything that was
said moving forward
I haven't always had a word for different
concepts but they were still real to me they still
existed
Once when I was told it might be good to set
boundaries, I was blinded by the filter
What I heard was "I can't stand you anymore"
What I saw was disgust
I had to worked really hard to be able to relive
my memories in my head without the filter
I know that's not what was said and what was
said was with love
I ripped that filter from my mind
I wasn't helping me anymore and though the
damage has been done
I can still appreciate what I have done for myself
I must.

Too Tight

When you feel everything so strongly
When I cannot breathe right
When I cannot sit
When you cannot make space
When I cannot laugh
When you cannot look at me
When you cry
I can only look at you
When you smile
When I cannot look at you

Kintsugi

I'm feeling so broken
My bungalow is here but you're not open
I'm feeling so low and it's almost like a show
down
Couldn't see it before I was too low down
It's hard for me to see anything right now, but I
know you'll be fine on your own
I know that you will be okay even if you're not
alone
I know that I'm home even without you here
I'm at peace knowing we are not each others
homes
Promise I won't pick up the phone
There's silence here but I'm not alone
I am at peace again even with the prospect of
never seeing you again
Hate does not take up the space the silence left
behind

Don't Say It If You Can't

There was a time when words didn't make sense
to me
When I couldn't write, and I couldn't count to
thirty-six
There was a time you told me not to say it, not to
say anything if I didn't first understand it
For too long of a time I didn't, but what was I
left with to say when there was still so much I
didn't understand
I wish you would've told me, taught me, helped
me
I wish you would've been the first person I knew
loved me…

Too Far Up

I think I am, and always have been scared of
heights
At the first opportunity given I have climbed
every ladder that has been presented to me
It is not scary climbing the ladder I smile the
whole way up
When I am at the top
When I have sat there for no longer than half of
a second, I stop breathing
And I would stay up there not breathing until I'd
lose consciousness and inevitably fall to the end
As I got older, I figured out a trick for when I get
to the top of the ladder
I close my eye, hold my breath, and then jump
and at the end I begin breathing again
Now I am smarter I don't climb ladders and I
don't want to
I sit with my loved ones and sometimes I
whisper, my voice gets really low, but they can
still hear me because I don't spend my time on
ladders anymore
I am scared of heights, but I am more scared of
not allowing my loved ones to see every side of
me.

Everything I Once Gave

I gave you time, even when I did not know how
much I had left
I gave you me
The best parts of me and they were not good
enough for you
I was not good enough for you
And with every breath I spent reassuring you
that I loved you I felt my heart receding
Maybe you were right maybe you felt it before I
even realized
Or maybe you were wrong, and I loved you so
much you couldn't even comprehend it
I think I loved you in a way that you didn't
understand
But I did love you
Do you understand?

Three Circles or More

When I was little, I wanted to be famous
I only ever thought that being famous meant that
you had a lot of friends
By that logic I am famous, and I am in love with
the paparazzi
They are the ones that take silly pictures of me
and videos of me when I'm feeling on top of the
world
They make me feel on top of the world
Logically speaking how much love can one
person give to others?
Is there a number at which you have to stop
because you are no longer able to maintain what
you have
I don't know
What I do know is that my heart is so big and so
full of love for my friends
I'm collecting stars and when it's dark far too
dark for me to see anything even when I try to
focus on the outline of something that I know is
there
I will have the light from my stars to shine on
me
They are my galaxy.

A Treat

For me a sour candy is a treat
For you a kiss a treat
So, when you told me that I deserved a treat I
wanted to run
It's not a treat
It's a disaster
One that will ruin me more than it will ever ruin
you
There's no hesitation for you
I envy that it's almost an innate response for you
It is not a treat for me, but I've come to find
seeing you smile is a treat for me
So, I will brace myself for cavities and bacteria
and pocket the list of benefits you sent to me on
that Friday
I like you so I will do this
I hope you don't see how scared this makes me I
don't think it would make you happy when I
anymore when I try
So, I'll be brave and I will tease you and you will
never truly know how hard this is for me
I'll keep it this way for you
A treat, on me…

Anger

I was born and there was Anger I've had him
with me all my life.
When I was 9, when I was 13, and even now as I
write this poem.
What do you do when the thing that fuels people
to terrible things is the one thing that has always
been with you?
Well, I've known him a long time, but recently I
learned how to communicate with him in
productive ways.
If the day comes and Anger leaves me, I'm not
sure I'd know how to be without him.
I try not to ponder that too much though there's
always something to be angry about,
SOMEONE to be angry FOR
So, I will let Anger stay.
He is not me and I am not him.
He is a guest within me.
If there is ever peace, I will talk to him.
I'll tell him I will be okay and that I know he
will still visit me.
Anger is with me now and so is Compassion and
Empathy
I wish that for everyone.